Spotlight Poets

DROPLETS OF COLOUR

Edited by

Sarah Andrew

First published in Great Britain in 2003 by
SPOTLIGHT POETS
Remus House, Coltsfoot Drive,
Peterborough, PE2 9JX
Telephone (01733) 898102
Fax (01733) 313524

All Rights Reserved

Copyright Contributors 2002

SB ISBN 1 84077 081 3

FOREWORD

As a nation of poetry writers and lovers, many of us are still surprisingly reluctant to go out and actually buy the books we cherish so much. Often when searching out the work of newer and less known authors it becomes a near impossible mission to track down the sort of books you require. In an effort to break away from the endless clutter of seemingly unrelated poems from authors we know nothing or little about; Spotlight Poets has opened up a doorway to something quite special.

Droplets Of Colour is a collection of poems to be cherished forever; featuring the work of ten captivating poets each with a selection of their very best work. Placing that alongside their own personal profile gives a complete feel for the way each author works, allowing for a clearer idea of the true feelings and reasoning behind the poems.

The poems and poets have been chosen and presented in a complementary anthology that offers a variety of ideals and ideas, capable of moving the heart, mind and soul of the reader.

Sarah Andrew

CONTENTS

Janet Cavill		1
	Villanelle	2
	Blue Lady	3
	Beyond The Horizon	4
	E Tenebris Lux	
	(Out Of Darkness Light)	5
	The Cornish Man	6
	Notice On Entering An Old Church	7
	The Lost Village	8
	Feline Friend	10
	My Darling Bride	11
	Our Love	12
Patricia Ann Bradley		13
	Love's Reward	14
	Willow	15
	Winter's Walk	16
	Seasons	17
	The Lost World	18
	Evergreens	19
	Wonders Of The Universe	20
	Man's Inhumanity	21
	The Thunderous Sky	22
	The World Around Us	23
	Emily	24
	Philippa	25
Hislun Credcane		26
	Crystal Rain	27
	Meet The Idiot	28
	Random	29
	A Girl For All Seasons	30
	From The Outside In	31
	The One Truth	32
	The Chase	33
	My Lady Of The Night	34

Mother/Daughter	35
Tunnel Vision	36
Shadows	37
The Mist On The Moor	38

Jon Oyster   40

Dyslexia Can Be Deadly	41
Jerry Jerry Jerry	42
Safe Science For Today	43
Nice Personality	44
My Favourite Audience	45
Modern Day Philosophy	46
Meeting	47
Maimed	48
Lobotomy	49
Educate Myself	50
Mirror, Mirror	51
Trains On Time	52
European Seduction	53

Robert Shooter   54

Inheritance Tacks	56
Repairing The Nets	57
Song And Dance	58
Oil	59
Psychology	60
Near Spurn Point	61
Process Theology	62
Mutate	63
Intermediate Object	64
Ocean's Spray	65
Tablets	66
Nesting	67
Catch 22	68
Choice	69
Getting There	70

Clovis Powell		71
	Where In The World	72
	Market Day	73
	Children	74
	A Way Of Life	75
	Park Walk	76
	Watch And Listen	77
	Someone	78
	High In The Sky	79
	Living On Diet	80
	Changes	81
	Coffee Bean	82
Ann Dutschak		83
	Peace	84
	Friendship	85
	Love	86
	Dreaming	87
	Price Of Love	88
	Christmas Time	89
	Loneliness	90
	Broken	91
	Blossoms Of Love	92
	Summertime	93
	Reborn	94
Patricia Heath		95
	Feeling Love	96
	The Flu	97
	Peter Pouting Plays Truant	98
	Reach	100
	Loving You	101
	My Finny	102
	Love Continues	103
	Somali Sister	104
	Wind Chimes	105
	In Memory Of Jack Waterhouse	106
	Sparrow	107

Kristina Howells		108
	A Prayer	109
	The Wild Flower	110
	The Wild Rose	111
	The Winds Chime	112
	Oriental Moon	113
	A Horse	114
	At The Races	115
	Lost	116
	The Lord Doth Move	117
	The Silence Is Killing Me	118
	Pain	119
	Lament	120
	The Future	123
Sandra Watton		124
	If We Could All Dream The Same	125
	War	126
	How I Want To Be	127
	On The Horizon	128
	This Is Our Day	129
	Tragic Sunday - 30/01/1972	130
	Night-Time Misery	131
	Heaven Was Missing Two Angels	132
	Kids From Coleraine Town	134
	The Last Sleep	135
	Love Is All Around	136

Janet Cavill

I was born in the Deane Valley in 1936 - and have lived and worked here all my life. I worked for many years in the Mental Health Service and enjoyed that work.

I am very happy and married to Roy. We both enjoy music and I am deputy organist at Watl Parish Church.

I enjoy writing about a variety of subjects, I enjoy writing on a religious theme - and about how people gain strength from love or from their every day life and their particular faith.

I attend a course in Creative Writing at Dearne Valley College, Watlon-Dearne, and have recently submitted a 'Note Book' on various types of stories and poems.

VILLANELLE

The night grows darker over yonder hill,
The sunshine awaits another day
The daylight fails, and all is still.

We saw the break of this most glorious day
The stars now shine to cheer our way
The night grows darker over yonder hill.

We lived to do our work, our lives to fill,
We toiled all day and on into the night,
The daylight fails, and all is still.

We saw the children playing by the stream
And life should be, but yet a dream,
The night grows darker over yonder hill.

And now at last, we take our rest
This night our sleep shall sure be blest.

The stillness of the night is now so nigh
Sweet dreams are there to see us through
The night grows darker over yonder hill,
The daylight fails, and all is still.

BLUE LADY

I gave her blue cornflowers,
Blue flowers for a blue lady.
Beautiful sweet smelling flowers,
For my blue lady.

She had blue eyes and a blue rinse,
A true blue lady.
She gathered bluebells from the woods,
Blue iris, hyacinth blue from her garden,
Blue glass from the shops.

Why was she a blue lady?
Love and joy were hers in good measure,
She just loved blue
All shades from powder to navy.

My blue lady just loves blue,
Blue everything adorns the house,
She is my blue lady.
Even when grey streaks shine in her hair,
She is forever my elegant blue lady.

BEYOND THE HORIZON

Beyond the horizon,
I see beyond the horizon,
Bright skies,
My love -
Children playing.

Beyond the horizon, I see -
No more sorrow,
No more warfare,
No more disasters,
No more drugs,
No more worry.

Beyond the horizon, I see -
All that is good,
A better land,
My loved ones,
I see my Lord and Saviour,
Waiting to greet me.
Waiting to bring me peace,
Peace, perfect peace.

E Tenebris Lux (Out Of Darkness Light)

What of the valley now the mines have gone?
What of the people who have to carry on?
Gone are the head stocks, the chimneys and the tips
Gone are the railroads, the wagons and the skips.

Deep underground, the silent caverns stand
But though the rocks by man's determined hand
Highways and byways down which the coal was brought
Destined for furnace, for homestead and for port.

Down in the darkness, there is no day or night
Never again the smallest spark of light
Never more a football, or a spoken word
Where once was noise and bustle, there's nothing to be heard.

Left as an underworld, that none shall see again
Sealed like a tomb forever to remain
A subject of legend and failing memory
Part of our folklore to be, eventually.

What of men who laboured in the mine?
As they grow old their stories will decline
Tales of disasters of strikes and honest toil
Now all replaced by natural gas and oil.

THE CORNISH MAN

Today I'm going to Cornwall
St Ives to be precise,
I'll go by train - the Cornish Man,
Will bear me on my way.

I'll walk and swim,
I'll eat and sleep,
I'll relax and I shall bathe
On a lovely Cornish beach my dear
I'll hold you close to me.

On glorious summer evenings
I'll wile away the time
I'll visit ancient churches
To thank God for these days.

I'll walk along the sea front
And hold on to your arm
I'll get to know you sweet one
I'll love you with my heart.

We've had a lovely wedding day
My darling one and I
Today's the day we speak of 'we'
And never more of 'I'.

Today we stood before God's altar
We must never, never falter.

NOTICE ON ENTERING AN OLD CHURCH

Good visitor when you enter here,
Pause a moment for a prayer.
For here our forebears knelt of old,
In peasant rags, and cloth of gold,
Lowly serf, and monarch's thane,
Each before his God the same.

The farmer with his 'farmer's lung,'
The miner with his cough.
The soldier limping with his crutch,
The child with whooping cough,
The widow grieving for her mate,
The mother with her child,
The troubled, seeking help and peace,
Each stayed a little while.

And so through plague and trouble,
The local people came.
To bring their problems to the Lord,
And call upon His name.

A Lost Village

Only the ford remains, to remind us that nearby,
Was once a place where dwelt a small community.
The grassy mounds which tax the walkers' feet
Were once thatched cottages beside a village street.

The ancient yews which grow beside the wood,
Are said to mark the place where once a chapel stood.
Long vanished now, the bake house and the mill,
The place where once the children played, is lone and still.

No stone upon another stands today,
To tell the fateful story of the day,
When weak and sick, a traveller there came,
A piteous sight, so ragged and so lame.

How they gave him succour, and let him sleep on the hay
And gave him food and coins to take upon his way.
Little did they realise, their good and kindly ways
Would bring upon their member, a terrible malaise.

The pestilence without a cure
Would smite both small and great,
A few would live to tell the tale,
Of their family's dreadful fate.

The village was abandoned,
And none came near to see
A place accursed of man and God
To all it seemed to be.

In time all signs were swept away,
And nature covered o'er,
A local legend handed down,
Remains, and nothing more.

On winter's nights a muffled bell
May be heard, old folks say.
A warning to would-be visitors
That it's best to keep away.

FELINE FRIEND

Oh thou the enigmatic member of the feline clan
Superior to the likes of man
Beholding all with that unblinking gaze
Silent of movement and of ways.

Whose ancestry pre-dates the Pharisee reign,
Worshipped by some, and yet by others slain
Thy dynasty has spread the world around
Wherever man has travelled thou art found.

Seeing, but unseen you softly tread,
Silent as the night when we're abed.

My Darling Bride

Come with me my loved one
To lands so far away
I'll get to know you loved one, and
Bear you on our way.

Today we'll go to Cornwall
St Ives to be precise,
You are so fair my Idwall
My one true paradise.

You are my Rose of Sharon
My lily - oh so sweet
Your hair, so sweetly auburn
Our lives together meet.

Today we stood before God's altar
We must never, never falter.

OUR LOVE

Love was in the air,
The night that I met you.
The moon shone so brightly
The stars from Heaven appeared.
It was a night I will remember
As I've remembered every night since.
Nights of passion, love, romance
Have filled our years together.

No longer in our youth today
Yet just as loving as ever.
Good times we've know - as well as bad
But we've come through together.

Our Diamond Day dawned yesterday
We're just as close as ever.

Patricia Ann Bradley

My name is Patricia Ann Bradley, the only daughter of Dorothy and Frederick Livesey. On leaving school I passed my entrance exam to the Bolton College of Art where I studied Art and Design. Then I trained to be a hair stylist and consequently owned three salons. I have two children Joanne and Gregory, who, like myself are artistic. They often worked in the art gallery and studio that I ran with my friend Carol. For the last nine years of my life I have devoted all my time to rescuing greyhounds that have been abandoned and cruelly treated when their racing life is over. Also I have done undercover work for the BBC, exposing the shady side of greyhound racing.

Recently I published a book of poems called 'Love's Reward' all about the dogs I have saved, some make you laugh, some make you cry, all make you think. The book was so popular it sold out immediately. My friend Carol Parkinson and I are currently working on a book called 'In the Shadow of an Angel', a publisher in London has approached us, so hopefully it will be on the bookshelves next year. Although I have been privileged to be able to do what I have wanted in life, and enjoyed it, nothing has given me greater satisfaction than rescuing the noblest dog, the greyhound. Seeing a light come on in those soulful eyes, gives me a feeling of job satisfaction. My book was written after Lexus my lurcher died, she paved the way in order that thousands like her found a second chance in life.

Through a lady called Rita Brydon, who I adopted Lexus off, I became the person I am today. She took me away from my profitable life as a singer and gave me something really worthwhile to do. I have been tired, but I am content, and it is with gratitude to Rita that I am the person I am today.

LOVE'S REWARD

I saw a glimpse of heaven,
Whilst in my bed last night.
It looked serene and beautiful,
Bathed in a golden night.
I heard a voice say, 'Come my child,
You have a job to do,
It isn't very easy,
But I'll take care of you.
The path is hard and rugged,
The hours are long and hard,
Don't worry I'll be with you,
You needn't feel so scared.
Just take my hand I'll guide you,
Along life's rocky road,
When you're broken, tired and weary,
I'll ease your heavy load.
If you help all the greyhounds,
Whippets, lurchers too,
When you come up to heaven,
This is what I'll do.
You'll have a place to call your own,
And all the dogs you've saved,
Will stand and wait so patiently,
Beside the golden gates.
I'll lead you to a paradise,
To rest with all your hounds.
Where angels guard you constantly,
And love and peace abounds.'

WILLOW

I'm cute and gorgeous, funny too
My name is Willow, how do you do?

My coat is all shiny, black as coal,
Mum says I resemble a baby foal.

I steal my mum's coffee out of her cup,
She's always calling me a 'mucky pup!'

I pinch off her plate when she answers the phone,
She really shouldn't leave her dinner alone.

I creep on her bed when she turns off the light,
I'm really quite an incredible sight.

'Now get off the bed', she says with mock scorn,
'You must be joking, I'm lovely and warm!'

Being a greyhound is hard you see
Unless you live at home like me.

WINTER'S WALK

I walked through endless fields of white
A wonderland of snow
Mist shrouded hilltops high above
A frozen path below
Imprinted footsteps followed me
Like ghosts that walked behind
A thousand dreams and fantasies
Re-echoed in my mind
The lanes transformed were blossoming
In snowflakes starkly white
The skies shone blue above my head
A dream of pure delight
A phantom dream in phantom world
But joy still ruled the day
Forgetting cold and heart's dismay
I sang along my way.

SEASONS

Swirling mist in forest glens, sunlight fighting through,
Shafts of light rest on the leaves, sprinkled with the dew.
Golden buttercups, daisies too dancing in the breeze,
Dragonflies, ladybirds, humming bumble bees.
Nature wakes up from its sleep, birds fly overhead,
Hedgehogs searching for their food on the forest bed.
April showers, buds of life, burst forth from every tree,
Spiders weave their patterned webs, like lacy filigree.
Then all too soon the summer's gone, and autumn follows on,
From leafy greens to reds and golds, and watery morning suns.
A yellow and crimson carpet, lines the forest bed,
Trees with barren branches, stretch out overhead.
Silently and gracefully, the snowflakes flurry down,
To shroud the trees in whiteness in winter's velvet gown.

THE LOST WORLD

Time on Earth is running out,
As man pollutes the air.
Rainforest, wildlife all extinct,
There is no future there.
Rivers of blood run deep and wide,
Famine, drought and disease.
All helped along by man's own hand,
With only himself to please.
Hunger, thirst, floods and life -
We are struggling hard to save.
While man's out quenching his desires,
His future he will pave.
The hardened few who struggle on,
To ease this saddened plight.
Will live to see another world,
Dry, barren, devoid of life . . .

EVERGREENS

Evergreen trees like lofty towers stand,
Vanilla and blue sky, cast light upon the land.
Embroidered on the landscape, flowers and trees,
Rambling down the hillside, hair blowing in the breeze.
Gladioli's sword shaped leaves, flowers vibrant red,
Rivers flowing through the land, bubbling waterbed.
Enticing perfume fills the air in nature's sweet abode,
Entwined around the hillside, bracken by the road.
Nectar taken by the bees, they hungrily devour,
Spectacular visions of beauty, in this my finest hour . . .

WONDERS OF THE UNIVERSE

The scent of roses fill the air,
A warm breeze on my face.
Walking through the woodland,
Devoid of human race.
Bluebells bow their bell-like heads,
The scent of pine trees sweet.
Lilies floating on the pond,
Moss beneath my feet.
I rest a while and look around,
At wonders everywhere.
And marvel at the hands of God,
Who created them with care.
We take for granted all we see,
Abuse our land, our air and sea.
It won't be long before men kill,
Our world, its contents, you and me.

MAN'S INHUMANITY

All that's safe and all that's sound,
Will soon be lifeless underground.
The sickening greed of human life,
Cuts through our souls just like a knife.
The chasm's wide, deep and sore,
Yet man is rotten to the core.
They love to kill and call it sport,
Compassion and love they all abort.
The tortured souls who's spirits rise,
Let our their pitiful, painful cries.
There'll come a time when man they'll meet,
Tearing limbs and flesh to eat.
Man should learn before his end,
To treat all animals as his friend.

THE THUNDEROUS SKY

Thunderous clouds hang in the sky,
Like billowing pillows drifting by.
Lightning, its jagged finger stretched
Across the sky, its knarled hand etched.
Rumbling thunder and torrents of rain,
Sweeping across the grassy plain.
Far in the distance, a shaft of gold light,
A rainbow of colours so vibrant and bright.
The thunder and lightning has faded away,
Leaving behind a bright summer's day.

THE WORLD AROUND US

Cascading down the mountain side,
Into a flowing stream.
The waterfall meanders down,
Just like a summer's dream.
Wild flowers in the hedgerows,
Their heads raised to the sun.
Dappled light on emerald leaves,
Rabbits on the run.
Acorns on the forest bed,
Conkers in the tree.
Spiders weave their patterned webs,
Like lacy filigree.
Rainbows spanning, arches high,
The smell of pine trees sweet.
Fiery sunsets in the sky,
Moss beneath my feet.
Stars like glittering diamonds shine,
In the heavens above.
All the world around us,
God created with his love.

EMILY

When first I saw your pretty face,
Framed with curly hair.
Rosebud mouth and button nose,
God made with special care.

I watched you grow into a girl,
Intelligent, bright and sweet.
Your nature is so beautiful,
To me you are complete.

As years pass by I wonder,
Will life be kind to you?
I hope and pray with all my heart,
You'll succeed in all you do.

PHILIPPA

Lovely as a summer's day,
Fresh of face and fair.
Blue eyes sparkle in the sun,
Honey blonde streaked hair.

Special child of yesterday,
My, how the years have flown.
From just a babe in mother's arms,
So quickly you have grown.

Your impish smile and cherub face,
Quite different from the rest.
God made you with his special hands,
To me simply the best.

Hislun Credcane

Hislun Credcane has been writing and performing for more years than he can pull a funny face at. He was born in Kent and is still alive, although he now lives in Somerset. He recently retired from the music business after 20 years of relative indifference and four failed marriages, but his desire to make his mark remains and provides the driving force behind his determination to write.

In tackling the themes of love, desire, happiness and the human condition, he hopes he may inspire people to great deeds or simply touch their soul in some small way. He hopes his work may also provide a source of spiritual consolation to the lost and lonely . . . and he should know. Whatever the case, it gives him the opportunity to confront his demons and give them a sound thrashing.

Outside of writing, Hislun still enjoys playing paradiddles on his legs, following his beloved Arsenal FC and various country pursuits like watching bees, talking to sheep and eating grass; all of which provide him with continued inspiration and an insight into the ways of the world. 'Most people are too wrapped up in themselves to notice what's going on around them, or lack the ability to put into words what they feel,' says Hislun, 'And that's where I come in.'

Future subjects for poems will include the increasing failure of British politicians to connect with their people, the philosophies of modern life in the Western world and how to charm a chaffinch with a breadstick. Hislun Credcane is not 96. So there.

CRYSTAL RAIN

She moves with the grace
Of a fleeting moment
Her purity so self-assured

Instinctively I respond
To her beauty and elegance
And all the promise that her spirit awakens

She yields
And I let her presence wash over me
As I bathe in its luxuriant form
Breathing her dreams
Never to return

She is as rare as crystal rain
Please world, be kind to her.

MEET THE IDIOT

Once again - a sad charade
A particularly unstable parade
Of my emotions
Caught up in the loneliness of introspection
In a feeble attempt to hide rejection
Yet kidding no one but myself

If a fool is a joker who doesn't realise he's a fool
Then a fool in love is simply an idiot

Random

The secret of eternal happiness
Is to possess the love of nature
And understand the nature of love
Because we all have different energies
And move in more ways
Than there are stars in the universe
So mysterious and amazing
It is truly a miracle of nature
That we are this way

Let us disengage from the daily persona
And leave it to grow old
Whilst we celebrate the ruling paradox of fate versus chaos
And rejoice in the unknown
For tomorrow we claim the future
And as we all know
Tomorrow never comes
Unless we live for today.

A Girl For All Seasons

There she stands
Such a pretty young thing
Covered in blossom
Like the first day of spring
Honeysuckle sweet
Just ripe for plucking
Summer sugar
But not for sucking
Taste the syrup
Of sensual yearning
Laced with flames
Of passion burning
Enjoy the autumn
In her eyes
For when they close
Her love dies
And heralds the winter.

FROM THE OUTSIDE IN

Just talking to you
And it all falls away
My whole existence
Reduced to the two of us

There's an aura about you
Something to suggest a deeper spirit
On a higher plane
Capable of inspiring me
To reach for the heavens

And though you'd probably say 'No -
I am not this person
Nor could I ever be
However much I try.'

I still choose to believe
That a time could exist
Where the two of us
Are alone in the same world
Making beautiful music together

Because sometimes
Love has to be this way

THE ONE TRUTH

I hear a voice, it whispers softly
Die! One day you'll die!
And although I know it speaks the truth
Sometimes I don't believe, however much I try
That one day I'll die

I'm not a manic depressive
In fact I'm naturally high
But there are days when I cannot escape
And feel compelled to scream and cry
Because one day I'll die

There's no hope of immortality
No eternity, the end is nigh
Except if you believe in whatever brand of God
A cheap 'ad for a pathetic lie
Because we all die

Regret is deep, it gnaws inside
What can you do but shrug and sigh
I'll strive to experience everything
Before I say goodbye

So when death calls and I happen to be home
I can look him straight in the eye -
I may be scared of many things in life
But I'm not afraid to die.

The Chase

Here it is, she says
I'm holding it with both hands
And when I let it go
I free your heart's desire

With gentle persuasion
Her hands give way
To release a beautiful butterfly
Such golden wings
        So delicate
                And soft
                       It flies up into the air
                           And far away

There it goes, she says
It's all your dreams come true
And all you have to do
Is catch it.

With your bare hands.

MY LADY OF THE NIGHT

My lady of the night
She turns to me and says -
I want you to take me home
This doesn't feel quite right
There are too many people here
And the lights are far too bright
I feel so much safer in the comfort of the night

When the moon is full and the stars are on fire
The path to heaven is easier to see
So take my hand and walk with me
We'll share our dreams and our desire
Let the romance and passion of night time inspire
We can leave the present and the past behind
Night's only dark if you are blind.

MOTHER/DAUGHTER

All that I have I owe to you
You gave me the foundations to build on
And a reason why I should

I may never be able to convey
The intensity or depth of my feelings for you
Inarticulate as I am with the spoken word
And here on Earth
You may never be rewarded with all that you deserve

But somewhere in the sky
I truly believe
A star burns just that little bit brighter
Because of you.

TUNNEL VISION

Will it always be like this
Destination unknown?

Travelling from one place to another
In the vain hope of fulfilment

My spirit transports me along a narrow track
To where my dreams are waiting to come true

My world has shrunk to fit me
And I'm struggling to escape
Another day underground

Climbing the walls to be free
Of the pain of wanting to be
Somewhere else with someone else
Instead of me

So I travel through life
To a chosen place
A chosen point in time
On a journey that some choose to call destiny
And I can interchange with intuition
If ever I doubt

But now more than ever
I need a loving hand to take mine
And lead me out of the tunnel
To where my dreams are waiting to come true.

SHADOWS

Oh to be your angel
To carry you far away
To never lay you down until you fall for me

Each time I glimpse
The azure of your deep blue eyes
I am captivated by their smile
Seduced by their warmth
Reduced to a quivering frame

And as I cower before your incandescence
Enraptured though I am
I still feel that the sun can shine for all eternity
And cast my shadow long
But all I'll ever be
Is just a silhouette
Compared to you

Because you are the angel
And I'm still chasing shadows.

THE MIST ON THE MOOR

I stand alone on the moor
Just a single silhouette on a distant hill
I can see for miles in every direction
Until the mist starts to fall
Slowly and deliberately
My vision fades
And I am swallowed whole

The last few days have been glorious
Summer sun to delight the senses
And night time rain to cool the heart
Lest it bursts with too much joy
Yet here I am
Lost in the mist on the moor

In the time it takes for my heart to miss a beat
I am engulfed
In an almost suffocating sheet of brilliant white
I try to see ahead
But only glimpse my hand
Outstretched in front
To find something familiar, comforting, warm
With which to combat the chill
To ease the wait
The weight of expectation
Hanging in the mist on the moor

I could perhaps advance
By resurrecting the spirit of my youth
And recalling the events of days gone by
The emotion invested within
And by using each memory as a stepping stone
To be re-lived and re-loved
Tread carefully, one step at a time
Through the mist on the moor

Because the alternative is to stay exactly where I am
And it's all too easy to remain stationary
In a world full of too many possibilities
And not enough opportunities
Overcome by frustration
Limited by fear
Feeling cheated by destiny

So I stand alone
And pray for the mist to clear
To allow me one last chance
To see the world at my feet
Before I make up my mind
Choose one direction
Start walking and never stop.

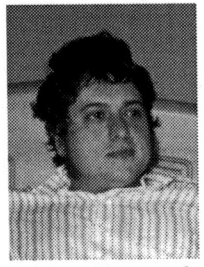

Jon Oyster

Jon has been performing on the London performance poetry circuit for around three years, he is also the MC for 'Walking The Dog' which is London's best attended monthly performance poetry event. As well as countless live performances, Jon won Carlton TV's Capital Woman (!) Poetry For The Underground Competition (judged by Wendy Cope and Roger McGough) with his unique take on London life entitled 'The Smoke.' He appeared on the BBC National Poetry Day programme, Culture-Fix, performing his piece 'Picasso' and has just finished filming for 'Beat Two' a show featuring new talent from the poetry scene.

You can hear Mr Oyster on The Poetry Society's 'Poetry Unplugged' CD, a live performance in Covent Garden's Poetry Café and on the Radge Poets CD entitled 'Radio Radge FM.'

Jon was a finalist in the West London Arts Board 'Dr Marten's' poetry competition and has had work published by The Forward Press, First Time, Monkey Kettle, Bad Poetry Quarterly, Unpublished, Poetry Now, TXT Magazine and Still Publications' on-line poetry magazine Jon's two self-published collections, 'Mein Kampervan' and 'The Importance Of Being Harnessed' have proved to be popular with performance poetry crowds and he is currently putting together a third anthology called 'Oyster's Oysters.'

I'll leave you now with the words of David Wardour (BBC Radio) . . .

'Very strong quirky material, with some great punchlines and payoffs. The material manages to avoid the obvious .. . The cumulative effect of having these poems relentlessly one after the other is very effective . . . This material confounds our expectations. My dyspeptic sense of humour and I enjoyed this very much.'

Hope you find a pearl among these oysters.

DYSLEXIA CAN BE DEADLY

Dyslexia can be deadly!
Getting ready for a date,
Didn't want to be late,
Vain attempts to make myself look great,
What I thought was
A cosmetic face mask
Turned out to be
A very uncosmetic
Mace Flask.
Major eye surgery later,
I arrived
Wearing my cheeks on my shoulders,
A very sensible jumper,
Chinoesque turned up peg top slacks
And clutching a prawn and mayonnaise sandwich.
She wanted to experiment
With a little M & S,
Or so I thought,
As she kissed a man clutching a cudgel.

JERRY JERRY JERRY

There are certain criteria
That one must fulfil
To appear on the Jerry Springer show.
The first being
That your wife must resemble
An eighties era darts player.

SAFE SCIENCE FOR TODAY

Here boy! Here boy!
See?
The dog comes and eats the food.

Remove the hound's legs!

Here boy! Here boy!
See?
The dog remains stationery.

Conclusion:
Limb amputation is an appetite suppressant.

NICE PERSONALITY

She had
A nice personality
It was
The fact she walked sideways
With
A prize pair of pinchers
Protruding from her panties
That put me off.
Oh, and
She did live in a rockpool.

MY FAVOURITE AUDIENCE

My favourite audience
Is made up of moles,
Well,
They dig whatever you do
Man.

MODERN DAY PHILOSOPHY

Remember,
The wise man
Says little and hears much.
The Morecombe man, however,
Is quite the opposite.

MEETING

After
Tense negotiations
We shook on it.
The moral of the story?
Don't conduct meetings
On mid cycle washing machines.

MAIMED

He claimed
I maimed him
By
Flicking a grain of sodium chloride
Into his eye.
Got two years for a salt.

LOBOTOMY

To relieve
The repetition
And the monotony
I gave myself
A frontal lobotomy.
All it took
Was the right book
And the right hook
To give myself
That permanent just done skag look.
Yeah,
Now I'll show those lawyers and doctors
And my neighbour Mrs Proctor,
I can really give them
A piece of my mind.

EDUCATE MYSELF

I decided
It was time
To educate
Myself.
I thought
I know
I'll read
The papers.
Three days later
I concluded:
You seen one Rizla,
You see 'em all.

MIRROR, MIRROR

Mirror mirror
On the wall
Who is the fairest
Of them all?

That man
Showering in bleach
I'd wager.

TRAINS ON TIME

You'll never get the trains to run on time!
A wholly impossible goal!
For
They require diesel, electricity or coal

'Quick Henry! Another Rolex for the furnace!

European Seduction

Need to be bein'
More European,

I attempted to seduce her
In German
She told me
I sounded like
A gurgling U bend
From a bad WWII flick.

I attempted to seduce her
In Flemish
She wiped it
From her left cheek.

I attempted to seduce her
In French
She wiped it
From the other cheek
And then reported a gas leak.

I attempted to seduce her
In Spanish
She told me
I sounded like a South West Londoner
Who just added O to everyo wordo likeo.

I attempted to seduce her in Dutch
She said
He can do Stephen Hawking, go on, do Stephen Hawking!

I didn't even go there with Swedish,
For she hated both Abba and meatballs.

Robert Shooter

I was born in Worksop, north Nottinghamshire in 1944. My sister and I were brought up in a loving home. We also had dogs, cats, chickens, pigs, tortoises, hedgehogs - to say nothing of an enormous greenhouse where we grew tomatoes for the market, and a large garden with vegetables, lawns and flowers where we could play. That the war and the doodle bombs were heading for Sheffield and Mum sheltering us under the Grand piano to protect us from them when they went silent, is my earliest memory. That the war somehow dislocated both family life and work and pleasure was also somehow apparent although my sister, being older, will remember more of that. We left this lovely house when I was nine to go to Creswell Colliery Village, in Derbyshire, where my parents ran a fish and chip shop. There was no garden there and my mum did pine for one. We only stayed there for two years and then moved to Mansfield, again in Nottinghamshire, to a house with a garden. My dad still lives in Mansfield aged 97.

Philippa and I met and married during social work training at Nottingham University. We have four grown up children and five grandchildren. We love music and singing in the Halle Choir.

Creative writing, which was encouraged at my school, by Tom Martin, the excellent English teacher, blossomed late for me. For writing poetry came as a surprise. My first being dragged out of me one Christmas Eve when I could not sleep!

This present collection, which I would like to dedicate to Margaret Duckworth, is from a reflection at Cleethorpes. My first published poem was adjudicated at their Festival winning its class. The connection with my parents - of their missing each other at Cleethorpes as depicted in one of the poems - does also happen to be true. Other poems are a mixture of truth and fantasy and I will leave it to you to decide which.

My poems tend to address the irony of life. They also reflect the deep pattern of nature with our world and our place within that. I hope they also reflect the nudging that God does.

I am a member of the Burnley WEA Writing Group. However, I can only attend spasmodically because of work, church and choir commitments. Having said that, this group is vital to me and I love it.

INHERITANCE TACKS

I circled round Cleethorpes six times
        finding good B and B
grotty pubs through to good hotels
        put the ladder down - gee

Rounders here began with my dad
        when then courting my mum
He travelled over the hundred miles
        to see here, her welcome

only to discover the coach
        carrying her choir had gone
returning early, class winning.
        He thought he'd got it wrong
and Mum not here for him at all
        so he drove back home too.
But Mum had waited for him -
        paddling in the sea; true.

She got the train back the next day
        singularly confused
was it off with him whom she loved?
        No rounders improved!

Repairing The Nets

He didn't come to Cleethorpes
to sing and fail

he came to talk with God
by the sea

eat freshly fried fish
in the open air

succeed in worship and praise
don't you see?

SONG AND DANCE

He thought again
he'd come to Cleethorpes to sing
did everything right
praised God in his element
sea, sun, sand
ponies, donkeys, birds.
Families happy, needs met
water and wine.
Will sing next time.

OIL

This song's far too good to have it spoil
to flow needs God's penetrating oil
a drop of his blood
as part of the flood
brings head of steam and timbre to boil.

Psychology

My for and against list useful
      of festival singing
might have been, if my whole being
      didn't send it winging.

Delusions deliver the goods,
      negatives sorted out
nothing but God can reach me here
      annihilated lout.

Would somebody shift that body
      off of that rotten cross
call him like Lazarus - knit whole
      again - yippee - not dross.

NEAR SPURN POINT
(To Miss Freeman teacher and friend)

With festivals he's got held up
        can't get beyond to see
crucified for coming second
        like for eternity

hadn't wanted to sing in this
        having free choice OK
she thought school would not put him in
        was he though - had his say

rebellion not meant - his nor school
        decision not to sing
backfired - she insisted. So he
        on a prayer and a wing

would school teacher drop him in it?
        Tell her - his choice - could sing?
On day his place better than school's
        she to teacher did fling.

Relief the teacher loves him so
        swallows the lie in quiet
'Yes we should have picked him to sing'
        said with such etiquette.

'If you'd listened to me' snarled voice
        'like - you could have come first,'
this at him with teacher also
        that bullet seemed the worst.

His spirit from that seemed so maimed
        still a thorn in the flesh
second in class of thirty pales
        with this ghost in the mesh.

PROCESS THEOLOGY

Self pity in the wet salt spray
        pounding on the hard sand
meeting the new incoming tide
        or was it pure joy? Stand

welcoming accepting his love
        for what is and will be
not for what could have been - was healed
        carrying, catching me.

MUTATE

Surprised that the class closed early
    on officials no blame
silly entrants that don't turn up
      such an excuse, so lame.

Yet their defensiveness fed mine
    fed that non-being form
annihilating circumstance
      fears returning as norm

without this feeding might have won
    kept silly fears away
overcome and not been undone
      been the ass that does bray.

INTERMEDIATE OBJECT

My colourful silly Limone tie
well celebrates
Lake Garda
remains
hot.

My Islay tie is a workaday one
every day wear
tweed reminder
places
love.

My Harris ties are strong like the crofters
wear for ever
subtle too
fibres
rich.

Why
Cleethorpes?
Never sing!
What might have been?
No tie! But freedom to untie some knots.

Some
link though
circles made
knotting parents
God getting it together womb and tomb.

Ties
that bind
and free life
remembering
love coming and going procreating.

OCEAN'S SPRAY

The tide came in to be with me
      sharing joyous craving
its crying on the sands salty
          crest lovingly waving.

TABLETS

One day
bringing down tablets of stone
glowing with creative vision

the next
presented with Hell's seething stagnation

opposition

keeping the pot boiling.

NESTING

The sea miles out
huge ships further away
hungry to see the world

birds nearby
feast on the wet sands

worms hide and make rings round themselves
trying to evade the birds

a man circles for hours
dithering where to build his nest
eventually
got a room with a view
of the sea and the ships
and came closer
to be with
the birds and the worms.

CATCH 22

Ought to sing and play piano
        use precious gifts without God
carrying me in weaknesses,
        like a permanent hod.

Could he not carry me in strength?
        Go solo and flow so?
Says he does in the Halle choir
        where I give it a go.

But there I am hidden with strength
        me lit one little bit
of the gigantic music whole
        but there I well do fit.

God said, laughed as he put me down,
        'I found you a safe place
        where I hear all of them and you
        humans producing grace.'

And I realised he was right
        that I could give and give
allowing him freedom to be.
        For music lets us live.

CHOICE

A pay day vow of poverty
      of praying for the poor
whilst booking in a good hotel
        with bath, sea-view, and more.

GETTING THERE

I think because God's carrying me
insisting that I talk to the sea
to worry is daft
centring a craft
whilst I learn to accept to be me.

Clovis Powell

I was born in Jamaica, the parish of St Elizabeth, the year 1945. The first child for my parents, I left school age 14 years, due to hardship from my mother's point of view. I worked in the field garden for nearly three years. I came to England age 17 years, the year 1962. My first two jobs were at the foundries, includes several more since then, my last job up-to-date was with London Transport as a bus driver from 1970 to 1987. I was attacked on duty twice and had to retire. Ever since I left school, I often think, what might had happened, had I been allowed to stay and finish my schooling. Whenever I hear about something important, and the word 'book' is mentioned, I feel I have to have one or I have to be there. I was listening to the radio, as I generally do, when I heard the advert about Anchor Books. I thought, that sounds interesting. I stayed by the radio for more than an hour until the advert was repeated. I wrote my first poem, Cricket - England Vs West Indies, and posted it off to Triumph House, Peterborough and Cricket - England Vs West Indies got published in an anthology. It has always been my ambition ever since I was at school to learn to read and write properly. I am presently at Ruskin College, in Oxford for one year, taking a course in creative writing and I hope to go on doing more studies in creative writing.

WHERE IN THE WORLD

We walk on the land
Night and day
We work and sing
And we pray
We swim in the sea
We come back out
We jump up in the air
We come back down
This land
Just had to be our own.

MARKET DAY

The stall owners
There at their corners
From early morning light
Until almost night
Where fresh things are found
All the year round
Some have rhyme
Some have juice
And they all
Are for good use
Brand new dishes here
Fishes out there
Things of different sort
For our comfort.

CHILDREN

Children cry
When children cannot defy
Children walk
And children talk
Children ride
Side by side
Children like the fun fair
Children are always near
Children sing
And children hear things
Children play
While elders pray.

A Way Of Life

Feet at the beat
Back at the attack
Facing the human race
Sweat and wet
Shoved and rubbed
Ups and down
Home and rest
It's a part of the test.

Park Walk

We walk
In the park
At summer time
Oh the feeling is fine
Felt the wind blow
Different smells
From lovely green leaves
Out of the park
Along the River Thames
We chat and joke
Free from fumes and smoke
Boat sails up, boats sails down
Just a part of London town.

WATCH AND LISTEN

Television and radio
One we view
Two we listen too
Pictures we've seen
Voices we've heard
Camera turning
Someone learning
Sometimes we get a laugh
From the other half
In the television studio
And on the radio
Two good combinations
Entertaining the nation.

SOMEONE

Jamaican woman
In an English garden
When the flowers bloom
May they freshen up your room
The day you catch that flight
You travel out of sight
Over hills and mountain
And across the sea
Wherever you are
You send sweet joy to me.

HIGH IN THE SKY

Birds fly so high
Those we see in the sky
The seeds birds dropped came out whole
Un-notice the seeds sank under our soil
Plant had grown
That we never sown
The birds ditched
The birds pitched
Could be that the birds had marked the place
There is certainly another race
The birds jump from branch to branch
In the trees at their own ranch
The birds had certainly flown
Many times over the crown.

LIVING ON DIET

Keep a regular check on the date
Weigh as a guide to the correct weight
Don't get angry
When you feel hungry
When it's not time to eat or drink
Keep occupied and have a good think
What they devour
Isn't our
Serve your meal
On stainless steel
Chew your food properly
Allow the food to be dissolved naturally.

CHANGES

Muddy waters moving along the stream
Eye catching as the shining sun gleams
Rushes, rises, fall and tor
Then the changes started to occur
The running muddy waters became clean
Passers-by stop to view the scene
People talk, watch and admire,
As if that's everyone's desire
Other things just stacked as if those on a shelf
As the running muddy water clears itself.

COFFEE BEAN

Seed bursts from its shrub
Showed no sigh of squeeze or rub
Plant grows and the leaves are green
Tree recognised as the coffee bean
Which bears fragrant white flowers
When it rains each got their showers
Then came the red, fresh berries
Some say they resemble cherries,
Which are harvested
And then tested
Parched, grind and boiled,
Some liked their coffee mild
In the coffee house what have they got?
Lovely, tasting coffee hot pot.

Ann Dutschak

Where do you start about how you got on to write poetry? Mother of four grown-up children, grandmother of three small boys, started to write poetry for a charity paper about 20 years ago, then got somepoems published in quite a few books.

Background: Just went to a primary school. I was born quite poor but I am not ashamed of that. I never passed for college. When the children grew up a bit, I started writing poetry. I got married 35 years ago to a brutal husband who bashed me about. The children might have suffered but I hope not. They are good people, who have got good jobs. Son Alan and his wife manage a newspaper shop. Daughter Kat is a window dressed. Daughter Maria works on a computer at a hospital getting beds for patients. Youngest daughter is trying to get into a nursery helping children. Aspirations when I was a small eight year old: I said to myself I would let people see what I could achieve.

Interests include: Knitting, painting, cooking, writing poetry, salt pastry.

PEACE

The birds are silent in the stillness of the night
The moon will give you the light
The stars will sparkle and shine bright
As the day draws to a close,
The sun goes down and keeps you warm
The promise of a new dawn
So put your arms around them Lord
Hold tight
Treasure what you have got
And think of others who had not.

Friendship

I've found a friend who's rare and true,
For me such friends are all too few,
Ready to share in trouble and strife
For that is what we go through in life.
Someone to talk to when in need of a break
And in their problems you try to partake
A helping hand reaches out to you
The sign of a friend so dear and true,
Having a special friend is rare
And you know in your heart that you can share.

LOVE

We have to let go, there's nothing to show,
Love is like waves on the shore,
No ripples for us anymore.
My feelings I'm trying to hide
Love has to flow with the tide,
It ebbs and we go our own ways,
You're gone and I'm left in a daze,
Love is rough and it's smooth
Now there's no one to soothe.

DREAMING

My dream is floating on a silver cloud
With golden edges all around
Through the rush of time
Higher, higher up we climb.
Bright and shining stars go by
Keeping up their pace we try
Awaking now, my mind a blur,
I wonder, did this dream occur?

PRICE OF LOVE

You don't need a coat to keep out the cold
Locked in a warm embrace ready to enfold
You don't need a watch to tell the time
As time stands still when you are mine.
You don't need a car as you walk through the park
And hear the singing of the lark.
You don't need diamonds to see the stars
Sparkle at night.
You don't need gold to see the moon shine bright,
You don't need all these things to make you feel good
Love conquers all knowing it would.

CHRISTMAS TIME

Seasons greetings has come around today.
Xmas holly around the door step inside you will see some more,
Scented candles around the room,
Light flickers casting shadows like a magic glow
Red and white wine starting to flow,
Turkey roasting in a dish,
Pull a wishbone to grant a wish,
Snowflakes fall out of the sky then slowly flutter down,
Shimmering when they hit the ground,
Then melting away till the next festive time comes to stay.

LONELINESS

I sit by my window in the flickering light
All is still and silent in the darkness of the night.
Not a soul in sight,
The only comfort are stars twinkling and bright.
Soon I will have to close my curtains,
Away from shadows and the moon shining bright,
What have I heard, footsteps coming along the path,
Maybe they have seen my light,
But they just disappear out of sight,
Dogs barking echo all around,
Then lost in the distance, with no sound
Time to draw the curtains and call it a day.
Maybe tomorrow someone will come and
Pay a visit - they will say.

BROKEN

My life is like a butterfly without wings,
Transparent to the touch, my friend has gone,
Her gentle touch, warmth of her smile,
My broken heart will mend
But it takes time.

BLOSSOMS OF LOVE

Love blossoms in spring
When birds start to sing.
It grows with the sun
When summer's begun.
It blossoms again but
Lacking the rain,
It withers and dies
Heartbreak and sighs.

Perhaps try again
Face the storm and the rain,
The droughts and the dews,
The blossom renews,
Nature's sublime
But takes its own time.

SUMMERTIME

How I wish summertime
Would come to stay
So I could brush
The cobwebs out the way.
Flowers taking their first peek,
Sunshine and petals with their
Warmth they seek.
Glistening with early morning dew,
To awake the silent few.
Everglades so golden and green
Such a delight to be seen.
Once more the seasons come around,
With all the beauty
Growing out the ground.

Reborn

The oak tree once so giant and tall,
Nature gives it season's call.
Time to shed its leaves
Gentle in the swaying breeze.
Acorns in a ring surround
Form a pattern on the ground
Leaves turn crisp and brown,
Then slowly flutter down.
Rings around count age gone by,
The tree once so strong must die.
Nature's cycle goes along
With the saplings tall and strong.

Patricia Heath

Hello, it's difficult to write about yourself, but I will give it a try. My name is Patricia Heath and I have two daughters, one son, four grandchildren, three big dogs and my partner Graham, who has managed to put up with me for 21 years. I work with people who have challenging behaviour and learning difficulties.

I have had a very hectic life but it is starting to slow down as the wrinkles are getting deeper. When I was younger I spent two years in America which I enjoyed very much, I've swam the channel in a relay team, been on a convoy to Romania, and been selected to fish for England three times. I enjoy going fishing with my partner who is a fishing coach and also works with people with challenging behaviour.

I have a very deep love for my family and also my dogs; I enjoy family meals, and like a good get together at Christmas. I love words, I enjoy reading and writing, and sometimes over a glass of red wine, I enjoy talking.

I hate unnecessary cruelty, it doesn't matter what to, I despise it: I hate people who are bullies. I hate seeing the rape of our planet through greed. I do not like people who leave rubbish wherever they are.

If I were rich I would look after as many animals as I could and would probably have ten Dobermans, as I love big dogs. I would also buy decent trainers and have the most natural garden I could.

I spent almost four years living on a very large houseboat; it was a wonderful experience and I would strongly recommend it to anyone who wants to get away from the stress of normal everyday living.

FEELING LOVE

Make me feel you love me,
More than love could ever be.
More than rain could ever fall,
To make a vast new sea.
Far more than all the blue,
That's painted in the sky.
More than all the tallest trees,
Whose branches reach so high.
I love you more than all the leaves,
On all the trees and shrubs,
And all the flowers in the spring
Showing off their precious buds.
I love you more than love itself,
Or love could ever be.
I'll love you for a million years,
Until infinity.

The Flu

I've got the flu, it arrived today,
From where it came, I cannot say.
It wasn't the postman who brought it to me,
It wasn't the pigeon sitting up in the tree.
Germs arrived at my house in quite a rush,
Headache, sore throat and a lovely hot flush.
First class delivery, not second class mail,
It arrived from the north like a northerly gale,
Paracetamol, hot water, lemon and honey,
All the ingredients, it's not very funny.
Muscles all aching, forehead in sweat,
Off to bed, I'll beat it yet.
Days without working, without any stress.
Whisky hot toddies, plenty of rest.
It must be the plague, my visitors say.
I want them all to stay away.
For when on their door the flu bug does tap.
They will say they got it from silly old Pat.

PETER POUTING PLAYS TRUANT

Penelope Plaice is ringing the bell to announce the start of school,
When everyone's there, the register, with all their names she'll call.
Most of the youngsters are rushing, so that they won't be late,
The last one in has the job of shutting the big school gate.
'Settle down' Penelope tells them, 'and sit down on your chairs,
You all must know where you go, you should be sitting in pairs.'
Sammy Shark and Colin Conger always sit together,
Linda Limpet sits with Lionel, he is her older brother.
The seahorses Kirsty and Megan sit away from all the boys,
For Calum, Jake and Kieran sometimes make lots of noise.
Billy Bass and Christopher Cod are both very late today,
They have found some rocks and puddles and decided they would play.
But they didn't look behind them to see who was standing near,
And suddenly a voice boomed out and filled their hearts with fear.
'What are you doing? You naughty boys' Mary Mullet said,
'Get off to school, you're very late.' Their faces went bright red.
They rushed passed Richa Wrasse, who was on her way to work,
She knew that they were always late so their lessons they could shirk.
Mary Mullet and Richa Wrasse watched as the boys ran into class,
Penelope Plaice was waiting; she had seen them through the glass.
'Take your seats, and after school you can stay behind,
Then you can do some spellings, I'm sure that you won't mind.'
The pair sat quietly at their desk and started on their sums,
They didn't want anymore trouble, especially with their mums.
Penelope Plaice asked the class if Peter Pouting had been seen,
'I saw him Miss' said Kirsty; 'he was playing in the stream.'
Peter Plouting is playing truant, he thinks he is very cool,
But without an education he will grow up to be a fool.
He will miss out on all the nice things that happen with school chums,
Like playing football in the playground, and getting top
                              marks for his sums.
Back at school Penelope Plaice has called everyone together,
'Tomorrow' she said, 'we will all go out, depending on the weather.

Bring some food to eat for lunch and also a drink as well,
I want you here in the playground at the very first ring of the bell.'
The following morning, everyone rushed to school, it was
such a lovely day.
They saw who was standing at the gate, it was friendly Raymond Ray.
All the youngest climbed upon his back, 'I'm excited' Megan said.
Peter Pouting wasn't there, he was still lying in his bed.
They went to Coral Mountain and Jilly Jellyfish, they all met,
She was the guardian of the fountains, which was a sight
they wouldn't forget.
The water danced and glittered and changed from blue to red,
There were beautiful flowers on the paths, 'Be careful where you tread,'
Jilly Jellyfish spoke softly and showed them wonderful things,
Crystals, pearls and diamonds, and fresh new gurgling springs.
They all felt very sad when the day came to an end,
They said goodbye to Jilly Jellyfish, they knew they'd made a friend.
When they got back to Rockpool Town, Peter Pouting was there,
He complained to all the youngsters that it wasn't very fair.
Mary Mullet heard him and took him by the collar,
'Then maybe this will teach you to come to school tomorrow,
Then you wouldn't miss the special treats the other youngsters had,
Let this be a lesson to you, not to be so bad.'
Peter Pouting felt so silly as he slowly walked away,
He knew that by playing truant, he had missed a special day.

REACH

I reach out my hands to touch you,
Run my fingers through your hair.
To gently touch your warm, soft cheek,
And I find that you're not there.
I snap back then, to reality
And know that I'm on my own.
For we have gone our separate ways,
Together, but yet alone.
But in my heart you will always stay,
A precious part of me.
Tied by ribbons finer than anyone can see.
For what we had is a secret and forever it must be.

LOVING YOU

Loving you is like finding a hidden garden, to open the gate and see the plush green grass, and smell the early morning dew still lingering as the warmth of the sun slides slowly over the horizon. To see the tall green trees swaying slightly in the warm summer breeze. To walk along the smooth, well groomed paths with the mingling smell of all the flowers gently opening their petals to welcome another day.
To sit by a rippling stream, gently winding its way over the plants and rocks, clean and fresh with a taste of purity.
I find the tallest and greenest tree and sit beneath its branches and listen to the birds softly calling to each other.
As the sun gets warmer I lay on the soft green grass and close my eyes, I become as one and I am surrounded by you and the feeling of love which flows and fills my whole being.
It brings me alive, it makes me tingle, and it excites me. It makes me warm and comfortable. It is mine, it is yours, and it is ours. We treasure it like a precious gem, nothing else is shaped like it, and nothing else radiates the colour.
It stands alone as we do.
It needs nothing to show it off because it is brilliant, it is perfect and it pleases.

My Finny

I walk along the road of loneliness, though even for a little while.
The road is empty, long and sad without your loving smile.
And though shadows pass so close to me, they never stop to touch,
This heart of mine that yearns for you, so very, very much.
I walk with head hung down, feeling pretty low,
Then I hear a soft voice whisper, 'Oh Pat, I love you so.'
I miss you as I would miss the sun, if it ceased to shine,
And wherever you tread and wherever you laugh,
                                      remember that you're mine.
To walk beside you all my life, in joy, with hands held tight.
To work beside you every day, and lay with you each night.
I'll hold your body close to me and run my fingers through your hair,
And whisper words of love to you and tell you how much I care.'
Your words, they make me strong again, and I hold my head up high.
And when the world is twisted I'll let problems pass me by.
For the strength of your love will see me through the sadness that I feel.
For the touch of your hand, though in my mind, make our love feel real.
My man, my Finny, I love you so, and nothing can ever sway,
This hungry need I have for you every single day.
For every day without you brings pain and agony.
I love you, please hurry home to me.

LOVE CONTINUES

I wandered through the valley to see if you were there,
The grass was dry and brittle; the trees were dark and bare.
I found you there that autumn day, beneath the old oak tree.
You held your head toward the sky, and then you looked at me.
I saw the sadness in your eyes, and pain was in my heart.
I knew my love that you would die and we would be apart.
The autumn turned to winter, the winter turned to spring.
The buds were ready, blooming; the birds were on the wing.
I went back to the valley, towards the old oak tree.
I walked toward your gravestone and sank down on my knees.
I loved you like no other; I loved you till the end.
Your life was full and happy, you lived it just for me.
You died for me as well love, beneath the old oak tree.
You died but memories linger on, you are still a part of me.
Although you're dead and buried, and I'm alive and well,
You left a part of you behind, our child, I named Michelle.
A child so full of love, a child so full of health,
With sparkling eyes to see the world, but not to see yourself.

SOMALI SISTER

How can I tell my Somali sisters that what's done to them is wrong,
When the tradition handed down to them can be so very strong?
How can I explain that circumcision is not needed?
I live in the west, I don't know best and would my words be heeded.
They should change their way, stand up and say,
You will not cut me open, no, not in this way.
How can I tell my sister who lives in the affluent land,
That tradition in my country has deep roots in the sand?
We have bright eyes and our clothes are gay,
But where is our passion that's been sliced away?
Tradition gave us infection and ruined so many lives,
For the sake of men and culture to make us docile wives.
I should have a choice and I should have a right,
But the women of my country are not ready for a fight.
We need education, we need to know so much more,
But the leaders of our country invest in civil war.
We need women of other lands to tell us what they know,
To speed up the learning process and let our people grow.

WIND CHIMES

Sit quietly by my grave for I know that you are there,
I hear the wind chimes in the trees and the breeze that blows your hair.
I am the light that will chase away the morning fear,
I am the wind that whispers gently in your ear.
I am the rain that will wash away all your sorrow,
I am the morning that will be with you tomorrow.
I am the sweet smelling fragrance of spring
That arouses the memories you keep hidden within.
I am the love that will never depart,
The longing and passion that once stirred your heart.
Sit by the shore and think of me
And remember things that used to be,
Don't let your heartache wipe away
The times we had, the special days.
Keep in your heart all the things we shared,
The love we had and how much we cared.
Sit by the shore and think of me
And remember all things that used to be.

IN MEMORY OF JACK WATERHOUSE

Don't look them in the eye Jack always used to say,
And if they start to talk to you, turn your head away.
They'll spoil your fishing by asking you rubbish,
And if your rod knocks it's the bite you will miss.
Find somewhere quiet to go where nobody walks,
Some place real private where people don't gawk.
Fort Vics the place he always said,
Yes, that's the place for me.
When the tide is right and the moon shines bright,
And it ripples on the sea.
With a rod in my hand and Jill by my side,
I'm the happiest man on the Isle of Wight.
I sit on my seat and my heartbeat is steady,
And when the tip moves, I'll always be ready.
Then I'll strike my bass and bring it aground,
The beat of my heart is the only sound
A flask of soup to keep me warm.
I'm not bothered about rain or storm,
I just like to sit here quietly,
My rod, my box and Jilly.
Yes, Jack said, Fort Vic, that's the place for me,
That's my favourite place I love to be.

SPARROW

I can hear them hiding in the bush,
If I go too close they all say shush.
Fast on the wing, always alert.
They hate my cats, that's such a cert.
The sparrow is a tiny thing,
But to the boatside they can cling.
Gale force eight is just a breeze,
Force ten might bring them to their knees.
Sweet on song, strong on guts,
They come to me, just for my nuts,
A piece of bread, cornflakes too.
Their whistle stops me feeling blue.
Your cats are old, one sings out loud,
But one day underneath a cloud,
His luck runs out, he closed his eyes,
And Tiffany has won her prize.

Kristina Howells

I first started writing poetry at Primary school. Since then, I have become a published author, and poet. The first book I wrote was on my local football team Luton Town football club, published by Bookcastle in 1997.

Then in 2001, Te Deum was published by Minerva press. This was the year writing poetry really began to come together, as I then started to see several of my poems published in Forward Press' poetry anthologies, along with two short stories in their New Fiction series and my next book Lettre de fatale published by Paragon Press 2002.

Poetry to me is like a painting that is reflected through words rather than on canvas. Pablo Picasso can be seen as a great poet, as well as a painter. This is because all of his paintings reflect love and life. The colours are portrayed in a surrealistic style, which can be shaped for the visual eye to make its own conclusions to the work.

The main reason for writing poetry is that it helps to link the mind to the heart. When you add them together, it makes a good combination for the poet to portray his or her own work like a painting, thus allowing the reader to see inside the poem itself, and to see the wonderful colours that the poet is portraying.

This collection I have put together reflects some aspects of life, love and passion. One of my interests is horse racing. I have included poems on this subject, linking it in with the theme of love, life and our very own existence.

A Prayer

Thank you Lord for the day
And for showing me the way
As I lay down to sleep
My soul becomes yours to keep
Watching over me till dawn
As the sun begins to warm
Thank you Lord for the new day
May you long continue to show me the way.

THE WILD FLOWER

The wild flower grew up all alone
to the sound of the wind's drone
sunlight allowed the flower to grow
when rain was used to sow.

The seed that let it bloom
growing up all too soon
the end is always nigh
as the flower wilts and dies.

Life is like a flower
except men can overwhelm you with their power
but love is a beautiful thing
like the flowers' swing.

The wild flower grew up alone
to the sound of the wind's drone
then the end was soon to be nigh
as the flower slowly wilts and dies.

THE WILD ROSE

The wild rose
that once stood
in the hills
amongst the brook

Looking down
from the branch
with its thistles
pointing to the ranch

The lovely rose
that never moans
even when it lies
amongst the stones

It's beautifully strewn
glistening in colour
the beautiful shade
of white and yellow

The colour of love
that's everlasting
amongst two souls
that from part of the casting

The wild rose
looking down
now never lonely
as it's seen around.

THE WINDS CHIME

He was lovely
Once was kind
Now I know
It wasn't him who caused the wind to chime

An enemy
Had come to revoke
Taunt and tease
Until the blood had stained the bloody coat

The wind moaned
But the trees
Stood still
The end of time was gunning for the kill

The battle won
Peace soon came
The enemy now gone
No more foes in the bloody game

He was lovely
Once was kind
I know
That it was him who caused the wind to chime.

ORIENTAL MOON

The moon does shine high
over the oriental sky
staring down at thee
smiling with glee

The horse so fair and strewn
has now arrived to our merry tune
she has come from afar
following the moon and the star

She is oriental in her name
as a friend rides her down the lane
oriental hears our call
when she is waiting in her stall.

A Horse

The horse standing in the field
not caring as he eats his meal
being watched from afar
he is going to be a rising star

A star that will soon be called to fight
a bloody battle with all his might
on a racecourse over the sticks
he is going to be one big hit

For now standing all alone
only hearing the wind's drone
as he is gracefully watched from afar
as he becomes a shining star.

AT THE RACES

Horses gallop from the stalls
jumping with glee
as the jockey calls
gee up there

As they race around the bend
the horses find their feet again
crowds cheering from afar
horses respond to the roar

The winning post now in sight
horses gallop faster
with all their might
as they reach the finishing line

It's all over in a flash
crowds throwing losing bets in the trash
now all over we come back again soon
to the sound of the horses' tune.

Lost

I am lost
lost within
the box that lies
deep within

All around
I do see
lost souls
staring down at me

Life is lost
gone and dead
he is buried
next to thee

I am lost
eternally
as all I see
darkness surrounding me.

THE LORD DOTH MOVE

The Lord doth move
in mysterious ways
he is there to soothe
the pain in our hearts always

I cried out no one came
lying in my sin again and again
death is near
I thought no one could hear

Until the lightness began to show through
God's love eventually came none but soon
in a man he doth show
he will never be a foe

All I can say is thank you Lord
now and for evermore
please don't hit me again with your sword
as I allow you into the core

I thank you Lord with all my heart
along life's road in a cart
let's all shout and praise His name
as life with Lord is no longer a game.

THE SILENCE IS KILLING ME

The silence is killing me
there's nothing I can do
I just wish he didn't have to flee

To a far away place by the sea
without leaving a clue
the silence is killing me

Was it meant to be?
I thought he was honest, didn't you?
I just wish he didn't have to flee

Love comes without a fee
he could have told me we were through
I just wish he didn't have to flee

I could follow him and make my plea
but it won't make it true love
the silence is killing me
I wish he didn't have to flee.

Pain

Pain, pain is all I feel
deep within my soul
I cry out, but no one cares
'Stop being silly,' is all I hear

Friends listen for a time
they get bored and flee
like a bird does whilst sitting on a tree
all alone without a sign

Pain, pain is what I cry
standing high above the sky
God it hurts
no one hears

I am lost
lost in life
there I am looking down
on a lost soul walking around.

LAMENT

'Oh no'
I did shout
when I threw
that bloody trout

It has come
back again
the end
that lies deep within

This illness
that plagues me so
why don't it
ever go?

One day
I will be free
from the pain
that surrounds thee

I am a woman
that has not sent
pain towards
my enemies tent

But why does it
plague me so?
The illness
that makes me low

I am afraid
I cannot say
as it's nothing
I hear again

It is, it is
hard to see
why oh why
has it happened to me?

One moment
I am high
living life
without a lie

Then the next
I am down
trying not
to fall to the ground

Soon, soon
I begin to cry
no one ever
hears my sigh

The letter
that I darest throw
trying to cope
with the blow

If it is not man
it's something else
why does life
affect my health?

Then I
eventually die
never have I
lived a lie

Was I nice?
I never hear
death came
and took me dear

'Oh no!'
I do shout
deep down the hole
with the bloody trout.

THE FUTURE

Mobile phones
Faxes to please
Communication
No longer seized

Letters through post
No longer the aim
As e-mails are sent
Instead of the same

Robots as pets
The future
Maybe
Soon to be vexed

Digital TV
Phone with a camera
For all to see
Soon will be the key

The future is ours
To do as we wish
Technology, changes
What next is on the list?

Sandra Watton

I'm a student at Causeway Institute of Higher Education; I'm also a trained bereavement counsellor and intent to study psychology at a higher level with Open University. I am a natural listener who loves to help those who need my help most, which is why I have chosen a career in the field of counselling and psychology; I suppose this way I can use my natural ability to help to its fullest potential.

I have only been writing poetry for the past 16 months but have already been published in six different anthologies; this of course has given me great confidence and motivation. I like to vary my stile of writing, but like any poet I have a favourite style which is mostly ironical and satirical. I suppose I get this from my idol Roger McGough. You haven't read good poetry until you've read Roger McGough.

I was born and reared here in my home town of Coleraine in County Londonderry, Northern Ireland. People may say some bad stuff about wee Northern Ireland and yes, they're within their rights to do so; I myself can too, having lost a dear friend to the 'troubles' but believe me, when I say it's not all bad and I owe a lot of my inspiration to it.

My hobbies include nights out, going on holiday (when I can afford it) walking and listening to my favourite music.

IF WE COULD ALL DREAM THE SAME

I had a dream
One November night
I dreamed our troubles
Were out of sight,
No war, no guns
No fatherless sons,
We were all happy
And we were all one,
There were no bombs
No victims no losers
No pain.
In my dream
We were all the same,
Then I woke up to the sound
Of the blustering rain
And once again
Reality came.
Then I thought to myself,
'Isn't it a shame'
And wouldn't it be grand
If we all dreamed the same
But in thee awakening
Day
Light
Rain.

War

If in a war
Our country fails us,
What happens to our land,
Our life?
And what happens
To our children
If our past is not forgiven?

Who after war
Will pause and remember
The lives the wars forsaken,
And who'll say a prayer
In years to come
For the lives
The war has taken?

How I Want To Be

Every day
I look at myself
And I know that I
Have to live with myself,

With my gutless lies
And dark black secrets
Of bygone times
In my days of weakness.

I see in me
Ugly things;
Guilt and hate
To me this brings

I want to live
In honesty
And see in me
What others see,

I want to earn
Honest respect
And always to hold
My head erect,

I want to die
Conscience free
And deserve to be
What others see.

ON THE HORIZON

If you sit on the beach
And look out to sea
On the horizon
Is where I'll be,

I'll do a little dance
I'll sing a little song,
I'll give a little wave
For you to come along.

If you've had enough
Of this hopeless life
Then come on out
And dance by my side,

On the fine blue line
Is where I'll be,
The fine blue line
Were the sky meets the sea.

THIS IS OUR DAY

Today is our day
You're looking rather well,
I see you glimpse
Across the room
But not my eyes you see.

I caught a little teardrop
As you turned to me and smiled,
My heart felt rather heavy
But only for a while.

You quietly whispered in my ear,
'I had to say goodbye,
For now and forever babe
It's only you and I.'

TRAGIC SUNDAY - 30/01/1972

Fourteen lives
Were sacrificed
Some were old,
Some were young
But all were murdered
By the gun.

They took a walk,
A little walk
To make a stand
Hand in hand
For what was once
Their Irish land.

Their destination
Was fair treatment,
Equal rights,
And simple freedom.

But their little walk
Was apprehended.
And their lives
That day were ended.

What now?
Except remember
And defend the lives
Surrendered.

NIGHT-TIME MISERY

In the stillness of the night
The young girl walks
An endless path,
Her clothes are torn
But her eyes still bright,
As she travels on
Through the night.

With dirty hair
And finger nails
Still she'll keep
Her hopeful gaze.

She'll walk and walk
For hours on end
With hope that the night
Will surely send,
A shining light
To reflect her peace
For she can no longer,
Apprehend,

But in her heart she knows
That the only light she'll see
Will be the light of day
Followed by night-time
Misery.

HEAVEN WAS MISSING TWO ANGELS

In the early morning cries
I heard that a mother
And child had died,

I rushed like a breeze
To be by their side
Through the trees
And bristles alike.

I saw a light
Like gold; so bright!
Then an angel was standing
There by my side.

It softly spoke
These words to me,
'Please don't cry
for them, for me;
They had to go
where they should be,
this is what heaven
has told to me
and has sent me here
to tell to thee.'

'Heaven was missing
two angels you see,
So don't be sad
for them, for me.'

I looked to the water banks
And I sighed a deep sigh,
I prayed, 'Dear Lord
Don't let me cry.'

And with that the light
Shone in my eyes;
It felt like a glimpse,
Of paradise.

Then I walked towards them
Without despair
Because peace and love
Touched all the air.

KIDS FROM COLERAINE TOWN

I watched as the kids
Played on the ground
There were laughs
And screams all around.

I asked the big kid,
'Are these kids happy
And happy to play here
In Coleraine town?'

He gave a laugh
As he turned around,
He said 'No way,
It's just something we do
From day to day.'

I thought to myself
As I walked away,
I suppose this role
I used to play
And I was that big kid
In many a way.

But was I that unhappy?
Did I feel that down
Because I lived here
In Coleraine town?

THE LAST SLEEP

Hush now baby,
I'll sing you a song,
Hush now baby
Let's get along,
Hush now baby
Please don't cry,
I've never been good
At lullabies.
Hush now baby,
Not a peep
Daddy's got to go
And get some sleep,
Daddy won't be here
Much longer my sweet,
So sleep for Daddy
And let Daddy sleep.

Love Is All Around

Distant dreams
Over distant seas,
Love is all around us
Like a warm summer's breeze.

Sun kissed lovers
Like sun kissed leaves
Can swoop us up,
Like the branches on a tree,
Briskly shivering
In the autumn breeze.

Spread your wings
Listen to the trees
Sail the seas
Feel the breeze.

Warm up to the sun
Relive your dreams,
Love is all around us
Or so it seems.